Selected Poems

John Glenday's first collection, *The Apple Ghost*,
won a Scottish Arts Council Book Award and his second,
Undark, was a Poetry Book Society Recommendation. *Grain*
(Picador, 2009), also a Poetry Book Society Recommendation,
was shortlisted for both the Ted Hughes Award and the Griffin
International Poetry Prize. His fourth collection, *The Golden
Mean*, also published by Picador, was shortlisted for the
Saltire Scottish Poetry Book of the Year and won
the 2015 Roehampton Poetry Prize.

T0371015

John Glenday

Selected Poems

PICADOR

First published 2020 by Picador
an imprint of Pan Macmillan
6 Briset Street, London EC1M 5NR
Associated companies throughout the world
www.panmacmillan.com

ISBN 978-1-5290-3771-5

Visit **www.picador.com** to read more about all our books
and to buy them. You will also find features, author interviews and
news of any author events, and you can sign up for e-newsletters
so that you're always first to hear about our new releases.

For Erika

*'. . . whatever is done
by only me is your doing . . .'*

Contents

from *The Apple Ghost*

from *Undark*

from *Grain*

from *mira*

Uncollected Poems

There's not a moment to lose.
        Speak now if you have something to say and sing
if there is nothing more that can be said.

Recite the names of the dead in no particular order.
        Talk in your sleep; talk while everyone else is sleeping.
Tell the one you love they're the one you love,

then tell the world you have been loved by them.
        I'm saying this to you out loud because each moment
is granted us only to be lost, and because it's lost

there's never a moment to lose. Nothing
        goes without saying. So go ahead, say it now,
but not just to yourself. The great silence is coming.

from *The Apple Ghost*

The Rise of Icarus

My father brought a German flying
helmet home from war. The summer I started
school I wore it constantly while I played

outside, or hunted through the radio
for heterodynes. He cut the hose for oxygen
when I swung it round my head at other boys.

Of course, it was too big, but I loved
the leather's warmth against my skull.
The rubber earcups hollowed out his words,

and distanced from the substance of my brain
his lectures on stealing matches, crossing roads,
or climbing haystacks in my Sunday clothes.

Once, in a dream, I pedalled a tiny plane
across our lawn; the tin propeller hoisted
me through the angled joists of air,

until the cabbages became like sprouts, then peas.
Below me, father dropped his bicycle and called
from the shadow of the house, frail as a child.

But I was much too high, too far away,
and glorying in the weightlessness of things.
So I watched him waving upwards soundlessly,

as the swelling sun beat down upon my wings.

Flounder Fishing

Without the lid on, it reminded me
Of his flat-prowed rowing boat. You'd have thought

I'd come across him dozing in the bilge's
Buttoned silk. We once caught fish enough to fill it.

A foul day. East wind. He held his face
Turned from the gusts; the taut line

Dug into a cigarette-stained hand.
I leaned across, tugging against his grip

To make him jump and laugh. Later we lost
Our anchor, rode the surf towards the shore.

The wind-blown spray drifted over us,
Settling on our lips, like blood.

2.

Like most keen fishers, he would not eat fish;
And those the neighbours didn't take

Flapped in an inch of water in our outhouse sink.
Later that evening, when I should have been asleep,

I crept back down to touch them; to draw blood
Upon the hidden prickles of their fins,

Then slide a finger in between the gills. Looping
The frilly garter where the hook had dragged,

I thrilled as the dying muscle gagged and pumped.
Their small, flat deaths held on to me, like love.

3.

I didn't mind the waste, it added voltage to delight.
The next day, when I placed those tile-like fishes

In the bin, I turned them belly up.
There they remained, forever smooth and shiny

In my mind – I saw them gleaming
As he sailed towards the fire –

And when I found his boat, split
Like a broom pod in the uncut grass,

I felt his fingers tugging,
Though they couldn't draw me in.

A Dream of Gliders

Father built an airfield in the garden yesterday,
And I
(Having ceased playing the enthusiastic child)
Laughed at him;
Told him the garden was too small.
He just pointed at the sky
Where silver wings drifted against
The bright blue air.
The hot air held them, and only held them;
Softly rocked them.
My brother caught two gliders with a magnet.

A curse on the dog in our dirty alley,
Which woke me rudely with its stupid bark;
Which dragged me back to
This building in an empty sky;
Which forced me to admit
Our garden could never have been big enough
After all.

Distant Relations

Great Uncle Jim ran off to sea;
but he didn't sail far. He stepped

headfirst from his whaler, blind drunk
on rum, in a dirty squall; and sank

through the tasselled carpet of God's
infinite grey room, never to be smelled again.

My grandmother wept into her embroidery
for her brother's short, cold life

thinking nothing of the voyage
she was doomed to make

through the mouths of worms
in a ship of grass, with her name

and times carved in the sail
no winds would bend; no gust could fill.

Aegeus

My son is coming
From over the sea.
The sea inside the woman.
The woman holding the clue of skin
Inside herself. She is also the maze;
My son is his own monster.
He must overcome the bull-headed man with goldfish eyes,
And the fish-gilled god with bull's fists,
To grow the mouth which will speak
Of a kingdom I can visit no more.
This is the wind
Which spins the gulls,
Whitens the brine,
Lifts my heart,
Swells the black sail.

The Closed Fist of the Exile

for Bridget

You crossed a floorless ocean in despair.
No stars betrayed the course; a sloppy tide
Heaved underneath a reddened moon. Astern,
The white road hissed, and darkened, and was gone.
True refugees bring nothing of the past, and so
You came, bare-handed and alone,
To a land of giants, where a stranger
With your blood spoke comfort
Through the vowels of an unknown tongue.
In sleep you frown and sigh. Your shell-whorled hands
Clasped shut against the ebbing dream,
Where an ocean softly tumbles through the dark.
A fist first built for grasping air
Takes time to learn the contours
Of the heart.

Incomplete Fixation

I think he looked like me
when he was young.
He said this self-portrait
was not his best, but the first
print he developed for himself.

You'll notice it was incompletely
fixed. Salts have remained
which, tarnished by the years,
have darkened the emulsion.
Permanence fell victim

to his youthful eagerness.
When he had struck his pose
and squeezed the bulb, he trapped
an innocence which now endures
no better in the album

than the man. Nothing is truly
fixed. That which seems so
is changing at the same rate
as ourselves. I wonder, when
he stooped to gauge the frame

and peered out through the lens
would he have seen
the bright, inverted space
where he would stand, and from
the edges, darkness crowding in?

The Apple Ghost

A musty smell of dampness filled the room
Where wrinkled green and yellow apples lay
On folded pages from an August newspaper.

She said:
'My husband brought them in, you understand,
Only a week or two before he died.
He never had much truck with waste, and
I can't bring myself to throw them out.
He passed away so soon . . .'

I understood then how the wonky kitchen door,
And the old Austin, settling upon its
Softened tyres in the wooden shed,
Were paying homage to the absence of his quiet hands.

In the late afternoon, I opened
Shallow cupboards where the sunlight leaned on
Shelf over shelf of apples, weightless with decay.
Beneath them, sheets of faded wallpaper
Showed ponies, prancing through a summer field.
This must have been the only daughter's room
Before she left for good.

I did not sleep well.

The old woman told me over breakfast
How the boards were sprung in that upper hall;
But I knew I had heard his footsteps in the night,
As he dragged his wasted body to the attic room
Where the angles of the roof slide through the walls,
And the fruit lay blighted by his helpless gaze.
I knew besides, that, had I crossed to the window
On the rug of moonlight,
I would have seen him down in the frosted garden,
Trying to hang the fruit back on the tree.

Silence

Slate green,
sky grey,
and muddy umbers
of alluvial sand.

The waves have come
in their borrowed coats.

They shelve to the ocean's
imperceptible decline;
then gently fall away
like other people's lives.

Like other people's
lives, unfolding
in curves of silence,
searching for an end.

We only hear them
when they break against
our world.

The Moth

If the past were an attic room
in an empty house,
though it is not;

and if memory took the form
of boxes hidden in the darkness
of the eaves; though I know

that memory is without form;
and if there were a tiny window
set in the wall of darkness;

though there is no window
and no darkness;
and if I were to feel

a moth stir, that had wings
without dust, like the skeletons
of leaves;

to struggle against
the window that is only a dream;
then I would wish

that a wish were a hand,
that a hand touched a stone,
and that stones might fly.

The House at Boreraig

after Reinhard Behrens

I'll not go to the house at Boreraig.
I've no desire to watch the stones
resign their gradual geometry;

and there's no comfort for me
in the song of the rowan, as it empties
the old seasons from its frame.

Instead, I'll wear these
tokens fixed to my conscience
like dead stoats on a fence:

1. a riddled copper bowl
    which bleeds in the late rain

2. a twist of barbed wire
    clogged with oily fleece

3. an eroded bread knife

4. a curl of bootsole
    smoothed by a child's foot; and

5. by the twisted lock,
    of the broken door,
    of the burned house of Boreraig;
    a key, infinitesimally
    turning in its hidden grave.

The Bright Cloud

after Samuel Palmer

What fragment of
eternity will he find with her
concealed between
the scent of hay
and darkness; where
the movement
of a hand might silence
for one stroke the heartbeat
of oblivion;
where her embrace
encompasses the sunlit heights,
the distant rain?

Wet Roofs

after Bill Brandt

A flight of gables climbs the buried hill.
The wet slates flare against the quartzy light,
and lead the eye towards a shadowed yard,

with its line of washing sagged by laundering rain.
Someone, somewhere inside those huddled
terraces, believed this rain would cease.

Beyond the line, a single window hangs distinct;
it's faded curtains only partly drawn.
That soiled shape lurking by the astragal

could be a mirror, or a cracked jug,
or a face. Somewhere there must be people;
somewhere unfathomed people; watching their

moments break against a sky as ponderous
as smoke; watching the persistent rain weigh down
upon the strings of houses, and the linen

moored to stone; watching daylight slip
from the glass; and their own reflections rise up
like muslin on the far side of their lives.

Making Things Dark

A dark wind lifts
the pages from my desk
and scatters them through the open window
to the pine woods
and the unlit fields.
There is no point in chasing after them.
I go back to my desk and begin again.

The shadow of the poem
darkens the paper.
The meaning darkens
in the shadow of the word.
Time absolves me
from the burden of the truth.

Why do I write? I write
to weight the pages
of my life.
Why do I write?
I write to make things dark.

Red Shift

Sunsets are spectacular
these days. Our skin burns painlessly
in the fly-sprung twilight.

When salmon flesh droops
crimson for the knife, we remember
the hanging poacher's blood,

slicker than asphalt.
Those small mountain poppies,
fragile as butterflies,

tremble in their cyanotic
beauty. Philosophers detachedly
remove the petals, saying:

Beauty is enhanced by transience.
The Physicists agree.
They have deduced

from blemishes upon the skeleton
of light, that something is leaving
our world.

The Song of the Woolly Mammoth

I remember how the pressure
of your belly bleached the grass.
In the photograph your eyes

appeared half closed.
I remember the smell of your spine, bruised
by the weight of darkness –

those craneflies
wearing out their little engines
on our wall.

I remember how you idly
swung your legs. The shadow of leaves
against a page.

You said they had found
a frozen mammoth in the tundra.
Fresh clover in its jaws.

Typography

At the presses, they grumble constantly
about the quality of ink; although this makes
the books more difficult to burn.
No fresh types issue from the rook-filled

foundries. Old characters are wearing back
towards ancestral runes.
The newspapers no longer convey information,
but generate a speculative philosophy

based on rumour, and the size of type.
The poor malnourished printers suffer dreadfully
with hacks. They tell us how painful
they find it, touching those long words.

Dog Days

We turned them loose
when food reserves were
almost done. Poor dogs.
Torn between hunger
and the memory of love,
they hung around until
the stones began to fall,
then slunk off to the mountains,
growing thin and sly.

This winter, when they hauled
our screaming baby from its pram
or snatched the chickens from their open coop,
they sloped back to the woods
reluctantly, almost apologetically.

They'll soon forget our smell
now that their rotting collars
have worked free.
But strangely, in the hollow
of the night, we often
hear the guide dogs
howling in their dreadful freedom.

Pottery

Grandfather collects potsherds
from ploughed fields behind the house.
Spring rain has made them gleam.

He says he cannot recall
whose fingers shaped the clay,
but each year pieces stubbornly

return, in lessening diameters.
Now he lines his room with tesserae
from their past. Bottle bottoms crook

the green light in a corner window.
Segments of pipe stem litter the coffee
table like the shattered ribs of some

extinct marsupial. He hands me
a splinter of oriental plate, where
a stranded lover waits

on a fractured bridge.
Someone, some day, he says,
will watch our lives go down like this.

A Difficult Colour

Think of it this way:
imagine a sea voyage. You have drawn
the boat up on the shingle for the night.
The water is barely luminous.
Someone points into the gloom. On the far hill
they are burning crofts.
The rain comes on again, but softly,
to preserve the sanctity of desecration.
You stand watching the reflections
tremble upon the water.
It's that sort of colour.

A Traditional Curse

When apoplexy
strikes, may you
not die.

May you revive
beneath a calm sky,
hanging larks,

freshly stamped turf.
May you retain
the breath to cry out

strongly; tasting
stale air
which dribbles

from your box
like colourless
sand.

And may somebody
lingering close by
hear you. The fool

whose village you burned,
picking earth
from his nails.

A Science Fiction Story

Embodiments or projections?
We couldn't tell, but they existed
as shadows in shackled energy;
a bell of effervescent air.

The spectra of cataracts rose
endlessly around them, seeking
invisibility in a stench of ozone.
We sensed the tang of metal on our tongues.

In humorous music-hall jargon
they described their parent world.
We watched the rain dimple and streak
the mud around their cage.

They said they had come to tell us
how our world would end.
We already knew.
They demonstrated therapeutic instruments

beyond our comprehension.
We considered abandoning the wheel.
They said they had not understood
they were too late. We signed

against the evil eye, turning for home.
Weeks later they persisted, translucent
and uncertain, wearing masks of rain;
but in the end, they faded back to gods again.

Goodbye

Goodbye to you in your Range Rovers.
Goodbye in your carts, on your
donkeys, and your blistered feet.
Goodbye to our finest corn,
our fattest cattle,

our hamstrung children.
When you pause to look back,
our eyes turn to salt,
seeing such wealth removed
from the belly of our land.

Goodbye to our full bellies.
When you are long away,
we will thank you for the single gift
you left behind – the spare
constraints of your tongue.

Those thin vowels and ashy consonants
are crumbling to nothing in our mouths.
Thank you for your good language,
which you taught us so that
we might understand goodbye.

from *Undark*

Famous Last Words

. . . repito por el órgano oral de tu silencio. César Vallejo

I am a column of silence, resonating where it touches
on our world;
reluctant as silk drawn from flesh, or a harp
singing in its cage of wind.

My tongue is shaped by the sibilants of grass
upon air,
stone against thorn.

In my mouth
the vowels age like seasons longing to become soil.

The trees with their arms laden.
The trees with empty hands.

I speak for the pause between waves,
for the night wind resting at the edges of itself
and the easy dissolution of clouds.

I speak for the snowfalls and the flecked granite,
for the mirrors clutching their people
of familiar smoke.

I speak for tomorrow's dust.

And I speak for my dark father, who floats face down in the slack shadow-waters of memory, his mouth rinsed clean of air.

I speak for want of silence.

Annunciation

And this was their appearance; they had the likeness of a man.
And every one had four faces, and every one had four wings.

We were discussing the construction of an angel's wings.
She'd found that old print of The Annunciation
where they arch above his head like an angry swan's
and cast down radiants of gold-coloured light on the hapless virgin.

She said feathers must mean angels were reptilian, essentially,
but if angels were fashioned on the lines of a god, as we were,
then surely they should be mammalian, and their wings, (if indeed
these are to be taken as more than mere bright conventions of artistry

like haloes, or the holy spirit hovering with a hawk's jizz)
their wings should be skin fixed on a framework of canted bone,
something like fruit bats or devils. *Quod erat demonstrandum*,
she said. *You know: qui mane oriebaris?*

She said that if angels had wings and if angels really were,
then in her opinion their wings would be like the wings of moths
which at rest lie open to display the stains of their stippled faith
like bark, or lichen, or wheatfields viewed from the air.

Angels hanker after light like moths, she said, but they hate the sun
and painlessly shed their talc. She said she imagined
if ever we touched them with our hands,
no matter how hard they tried, they would never quite fly again.

Nimbus

i.m. Davy Brown

In Tibetan Buddhism, the symbol for the mind's creative power
is not a light bulb, as in the *Beano*, but a cloud.
And I've heard that in Mexico they believe the dead
may speak from their graves for a short while after rain.
But Skye is nothing like Mexico.
They would never fall silent here.
Then perhaps it's true.

When I was seven, my father explained
how the dead converse through the telegraph wires
and it's only because we're stuck with being alive
that we can't understand what they say.
When I hugged the pole with him and listened,
their speech was thin and distant, but as heavenly as song.

A friend once described how he stood above Bernisdale
in a winter storm and watched the waves beat themselves
white against the gale, then surge up into the sky and disappear.
He said a blackface ewe went floundering past his door like
    tumbleweed.

I believe whatever has been done can only be translated, never
    undone.
That day, rain tasted salt at Invermoriston.

A Day at the Seaside

We're out in my father's boat and he's fishing.
He's fishing until the daylight goes.
It's the end of the season and I'm in the stern
to watch for the ebb that would pull us

out past the Buddon Light and the mouth of the river.
But I'm not watching the tide,
I'm watching him as he fishes, because I've never
seen him so focussed before – so engaged.

It's as if the fish had hooked him. Then just
as he makes his final cast, an oystercatcher calls
far out across the water. Far out across
the water an oystercatcher calls

just once, and then just once again, and then its silence calls.
The hurt lies not in the cross, but in the nails.

The Autumn Ghosts

There are no ghosts. Life
spirals into stillness round an armature
of dust. (You may have noticed

how a people of ragged smoke
drift through the corridors
of memory, beckoning silently?

These shapes are of no consequence –
they cast the frail skin
of the present tense

quite painlessly.) There are
no ghosts. Listen,
it was only the living that you heard

last night, as they called out
quietly in the oblique, dark rain.
Listen, they meant us no harm,

they will never return.
They were haunting the graves
of summers they would live again.

Edie's Room

for Mary Stewart

Just before dawn, I was woken
by the soft hush of the dead about their work.
It was cold in her room; so cold

I could see the half-bright cloud of my life
hung out in the air between the darkness
and the moon. I can't help but fall

for the dark each time it has to go.
Its death, like any other death, leads on
from mystery towards brighter mystery.

Inheritance

Forgive me, time,
the shell of my son,
who will break on the wheel of flowers,

though you half fill
my hand with your hand,
you will always be alone.

Forgive me, time,
who smile and gesture from
your tumbril of fishboxes and string;

whose trusting shadow
drifts through my shadow,
as spawn through a shrinking pool.

Forgive me, time,
who worship my inconstancies
on the fail shrine

of innocence.
I was your man-faced god,
but I built my own feet from clay.

Jacob's Story

The humane man loves mountains, and the love of stones
has the same meaning. – Confucius

To sleep with nothing but stone
between our heads and the stones which beat
at the centre of the Earth.

To sleep against silence,
wound in linen as cold as the moon,
the skull clean as a driven moon, and then suddenly

to dream of or understand that laborious commerce
of angels, who carry between worlds
their baggage of uselessly beating wings.

To sleep as the dead would sleep (if only
we would let them sleep),
with the head on its pillow of naked stone,
but imagining the heart.

Fire Damp

And yet, I believe something
must sing in the heart.

I once read that when canaries
were taken underground

they would often sing back
towards what little light there was.

Portage

We carry the dead in our hands.
There is no other way.

The dead are not carried in our memories. They died
in another age, long before this moment.
We shape them from the wounds
they left on the inanimate,
ourselves. As in the fall of water – its persistence
wearing stone into a bowl.

There is no room in our hearts
for the dead, though we often imagine that there is,
or wish it to be so,
to preserve them in our warmth,
our sweet darkness, where their fists
might pummel the soft contours of our love.
And though we might like to think
that they would call out to us, they could never do so,
being there. They would never dare to speak,
lest their mouths, our names, fill
quietly with blood.

We carry the dead in our hands
as we might carry water – with a careful,
reverential tread.
There is no other way.

How easily, how easily their faces spill.

Concerning the Atoms of the Soul

Someone explained once how the pieces of what we are
fall downwards at the same rate
as the Universe.
The atoms of us, falling towards the centre

of whatever everything is. And we don't see it.
We only sense their slight drag in the lifting hand.
That's what weight is, that communal process of falling.
Furthermore, these atoms carry hooks, like burrs,

hooks catching like hooks, like clinging to like,
that's what keeps us from becoming something else,
and why in early love, we sometimes
feel the tug of the heart snagging against another's heart.

Only the atoms of the soul are perfect spheres
with no means of holding on to the world
or perhaps no need for holding on,
and so they fall through our lives catching

against nothing, like perfect rain,
and in the end, he wrote, mix in that common well of light
at the centre of whatever the suspected
centre is, or might have been.

Concerning Shadows

We all cast shadows,
even the sun, perhaps.
Only shadows have no shadows.
Shadows cast us.

Normally the shadow lies prone –
its grave is the sunlight –
but sometimes we may come upon it
leaning against a wall
with its limbs broken.

There are no shadows inside shadows.
Shadows are barren,
though we may contain shadows
as shadows may contain us.

Our shadows are no paler in the moonlight,
only we are.

Nothing can injure shadows,
but when floated on water
even a feather will crack them.

It's only when we lie down that our shadows fit.

Shadows are as gentle
and momentary as snow.

They can't thrive without light,
but light also withers them.
In this respect, they resemble people.

Be careful:
always keep yourself between
your shadow and the sun.

At Barry Mill

I wish I could be chaff. I like chaff best of all.
Closer to dust than bread,
chaff drifts downwind of the beaten seed
and as with the soul – our heart's chaff – sails

for a moment through its banister of light.
Deep in the workings of the heart stone turns on stone
and those stones are milled by the flow of the constant grain.
But I'll settle for chaff. I hanker after things that have no weight.

A Nest of Boxes

*'This is Natures nest of Boxes; The Heavens contain the Earth,
the Earth, Cities, Cities, Men. And all these are Concentrique;
the common center to them all, is decay, ruine;'*
John Donne, *Devotions*

The heavens contain the earth,
and in the heart
of the earth beats

the ocean, and in the warm
hollows of the ocean
a child dreams,

and at the very core
of his dream
the heavens turn

on the axis
of a further dream
– dreaming that they lie

distant from the world;
dreaming how they will never
need to fall.

Nettles

Between the hearthstone
and the machair,

between the prefabs
and the factory,

between the bleachfields
and the river,

between the rhubarb
and the bicycle,

we are struck down
and we rise up again.

No hand dares touch us.
No one will honour us.

We are our own gods.

Alba

Some say she looks like an old witch,
a dark caillich with a cat's-tail of islands for hair.
Brine sluices the words from her cracked lips.
I say no. I say she's as fresh as these flakes
of schist and quartzite I gathered yesterday.

Some say she's barren: *'Look how they scoured*
her bairns from her womb with a dab of wool,' they say,
'and them scarce halfways down the road to birth.
The four airts buried them.
Their cries will circle the earth like little storms.'
I say no. I say she's poor but whole and strong
and I've heard her children sing out in our half-dark street,
barely a whisper before night.

Some say she's bad news, a temptress, a whistler on ships,
that the man who sleeps with her will wake one morning
at dusk on a hillside under the brisk rain, his pockets weighted
    with sand.
I say no. I say, look at me: I've slept with her all the nights of my
    life
and still each morning when I wake I find her tongue in my
    mouth.

Undark

And so they come back, those girls who painted
the watch dials luminous, and died.

They come back and their hands glow and their lips
and hair and their footprints gleam in the past like alien snow.

It was as if what shone in them once had broken free
and burned through the cotton of their lives.

And I want to know this: I want to know how they came to believe
that something so beautiful could ever have turned out right,

but though they open their mouths to answer me,
all I can hear is light.

The Ngong Peony

'We have not succeeded in growing peonies in Africa,' he said,
'and shall not do so till we manage to make an imported bulb
flower here, and can take the seed from that flower.
This is how we got delphinium into the colony . . .'

This is the truth:
Blixen brought with her into Africa
the *Duchesse de Nemours*,
a 'rich and noble' peony which bloomed
once from a solitary head,
magically huge and pale.

The light seemed to condense around its globe
which rose through a ground
of dark, lush, curvilinear leaves.
It thrived as none other had before,
nor ever would again, in all that continent.

She picked it, of course,
and within four days
it had laid its brilliance on her carpet,
shell by shell.

But it sang in those days,
it sang as the cicada sings
when it draws out the brief chord of its joy,
burnishing the daylight from itself: that carapace,
these words, this overwhelming dusk.

The Empire of Lights

After Magritte: L'Empire des Lumières, *1954*

The past is the antithesis of burglary. Imagine
a house in darkness. Or to be more precise,
imagine darkness in a house. Something akin

to that Magritte where the light is held
at tree's length by a clutch of tungsten bulbs.
The looming woods proofed with shadow thicker than tar.

In the House of the Past we move backwards
from room to room, forever closing doors
on ourselves, always closing doors.

In each room, we leave some of those little trinkets
we love most, that the house is stealing from us.
Because we cherish them, we abandon them

to the furniture of strangers. Wherever we go
the doors swing shut behind us without a sound,
and the dust drifts up into the ceiling like smoke.

Oh there is so much we would love to hold on to,
but so little room. If only we could come back,
if only we could come back in the morning,

things would be so much better. But on we must go,
creeping backwards through silent bedrooms,
closing doors quietly for fear of waking ourselves.

Emptying our pockets, emptying our hands. Heavy
with emptiness, we crouch down at last in the lee
of a shattered window, where we dream of those

ancient burdens, long resolved. And the fragments
of glass fidget like broken insects on the rug,
eager to heal where our fists will gently touch.

Son of Man

After Magritte: Le fils de l'homme, *1964*

There are times
when in the most unhindered light
we can discern shadows

cast by something less
than visible. Imprints or absences
our bodies, somehow, lie beyond.

There are times when history
flows through us
like a trembling music,

as though, invested
with the sea, we had ourselves
become an instrument.

And there are times
when all our weaknesses hang
ripening between us

and ourselves. Those ancient,
unencompassed frailties we could not look
beyond, nor hide behind.

The Song of the Violet

After Magritte: Le chant de la violette, *1951*

There is a special dust which gathers in the heart
on winter afternoons: the last of the daylight
thins to a distant thrum, whatever of myself I saw
as false suddenly becomes unknown, luminous or true.
But the moment dies, it burns through the lining
of the soul like joy and its passing,

its passing puts the death and life in me.
If we were free once, we were free, and being free,
traded that freedom for this,
because we wanted more – more than a choice,
more than mere absence of despair –
the brilliance and the savagery of one squandered hour.

Over Vitebsk

After Chagall

Grandfather came home early from a war
that had never been. I remember he looked
quite regimental in his winter coat

and battered postman's cap, as he dangled
like gathered smoke between the rooftops
and the sky. I was roused by the rap

of his white stick on our slates. Behind me
a voice hissed: *'He's calling
our names, I think. Listen!'*

And I think he was: softly at first, but quite
insistently. The moon of his face bleached
green by the chlorine gas and cold.

Then suddenly nothing seemed straight
any more. Dawn spiralled in flames.
Snow curved through the runnel of our street.

The Market Square (no longer square)
had gently liquefied into a milky lens.
Even the steeple where he moored himself

was yawing crazily above its arc of little graves.
He called out again with greater urgency,
and not just our names, but something like:

. . . something *'man'* and then *'land'* and then something
'gone' . . . Though we craned in the yard with our ears
cupped, we still couldn't make him out.

The youngsters lobbed rocks and insults
as he raved: *'Where's your rifle, Grandad?'*
'Show us a skull!'

Gobs of spittle began to drench us – they reeked
of a thin despair – so we wafted our caps and bonnets,
winnowed his chaff away.

'Peace at last, praise God,' whispered Nana,
crossing herself again, as the last few strands
of his message darkened the earth, like rain.

from *Grain*

Epitaph

Father, forgive this man.
He never listened to your song
till it was all but done
then found he couldn't sing the words
so he spoke the tune.

Imagine You are Driving

Imagine you are driving
nowhere, with no one beside you;
with the empty road unravelling and ravelling
in sympathy as the wheel turns in your hands.

On either side the wheatfields go shimmering
past in an absence of birdsong, and the sky
decants the shadows of the weather from itself.
So you drive on, hopeful of a time

when the ocean will rise up before you like dusk
and you will make landfall at last –
some ancient, long-forgotten mooring,
which both of you, of course, will recognize

though as I said before, there is no one beside you
and neither of you has anywhere to go.

The River

This is my formula for the fall of things:
we come to a river we always knew we'd have to cross.
It ferries the twilight down through fieldworks

of corn and half-blown sunflowers.
The only sounds, one lost cicada calling to itself
and the piping of a bird that will never have a name.

Now tell me there is a pause
where we know there should be an end;
then tell me you too imagined it this way

with our shadows never quite touching the river
and the river never quite reaching the sea.

At Innernytie

for Gail and Sandy Wylie

All we can ever hear
is the slipping by of things
as another night comes down.

Everything changes forever;
everything remains.
The elderflower moon

the rapefield's cadmium
and the lark's voice,
widening into silence like a river.

Listen:
beyond the heart's breath
and the lingering soul,

beyond the last bee
dying in the honeysuckle,
beyond the cirrus and the fallstreaks

of tomorrow's rain –
the sound of things becoming
what they never will again.

Landscape with Flying Man

I read about him that was given wings.
His father fixed those wings to carry him away.

They carried him halfway home, and then he fell.
And he fell not because he flew

but because he loved it so. You see
it's neither pride, nor gravity, but love

that pulls us back down to the world.
Love furnishes the wings, and that same love

will watch over us as we drown.
The soul makes a thousand crossings, the heart, just one.

Etching of a Line of Trees

i.m. John Goodfellow Glenday

I carved out the careful absence of a hill and a hill grew.
I cut away the fabric of the trees
and the trees stood shivering in the darkness.

When I had burned off the last syllables of wind,
a fresh wind rose and lingered.
But because I could not bring myself

to remove you from that hill,
you are no longer there. How wonderful it is
that neither of us managed to survive

when it was love that surely pulled the burr
and love that gnawed its own shape from the burnished air
and love that shaped that absent wind against a tree.

Some shadow's hands moved with my hands
and everything I touched was turned to darkness
and everything I could not touch was light.

St Orage

Preserve us, St Orage, you whose image stares down
on our weed-snagged railway sidings and choked
factory yards; whose relics crumble in a cardboard box
in a hampered lock-up somewhere. We await your word.

St Eadfast and St Alwart, we rely on you
to indicate the Good Path, however stony.
Lead us not into that rock-strewn gully
clogged with St Randed's bones.

O Lord, we know your faithful
knew more deaths than we had fingers –
St Ifle and St Rangle and St Arving and St Ab, all
flew into your mercy through their disparate anguishes.

But most of all, remember us yourselves,
forgotten saints we here commemorate:
St Agger of the drunken brawling praise;
St Ainless, martyred on the lopped branch of his perfect life;

St Anza, stunned by her own reverberating song;
and blameless, maculate St Igmata, dead and forgiving child,
who even in the crib, they say, held up her little punctured hands
in wonder and in ignorance, and cried.

A Fairy Tale

She had been living happily ever before,
waltzing through imagined ballrooms in the arms
of a handsome young prince. Then, one day, they kiss
for the first time, he takes back the word love

and suddenly bloats to an idle, wounded beast
that stoops above her in its thickening hide.
She trembles before his laboured breath and white, strange eyes.
Each night from her solitary bed, she overhears the echoes

of unimaginable rages which transform their castle
to a ruin of shadowy rooms with a cursed and sleeping heart.
At last she understands him poorly enough to be terrified
and run a gauntlet of scattering wolves to the arms of her sick father

who greets her with a tearful goodbye. They subsist
forever after on a diet of simple gruel and vague desire.
When passers-by ask her about her life, she waltzes the laundry
to her heart and answers with a distant smile: *Once upon a time.*

The Man Rats Loved

That wasn't much of a tune you played:
just a few sour notes fingered for your own pleasure

as you pranced through my childhood
(such a meagre town) half dressed as the mother,

half as the father and neither half fitting right.
I didn't fall for you, but followed anyway, eager

enough to trust my luck wherever you might lead,
under the hill or into the swollen river.

Valentine

suck my red heart white, I will, because I love you, bless me,
o, and here, I will say, see I am back, in spite of you to bring
a gift I grew, it was busy in me once, filled the red branch
with blood, knocking like hope, and beat time to my life's
decline, then followed after in its way, and did its duty.

The Afterlife

Because I could I did – build her I mean – from bits I found,
the scraps of being no one else would have – harvested organs,
glands that set the balance, patchwork features still the shape
of who they were before they weren't, all hooked to a sack of
blood and made to go somewhat. Bones hinged in their proper
order, muscles flinched, the milk set in her eyes (a close match,
not a pair). Somehow it worked. A marvel. God knows how.
You should have seen me hook the weather at its worst, all
broken lights and wattage, then earth the brilliance through her.
Took this for a show of love though she kicked with a reek of
burn. It straddled every sinew, grounded at last in her opening
face. One lid went back, she gazed up through my downward
gaze, through the scaffolding of lights and instruments, on into
overarching mirk. Then just as the current died the grey rag of
her lips tore open for a moment and the air, forced through her
throat's reed, broke with a play of notes, almost like song

The Kelp Eaters

Hydrodamalis gigas

These beasts are four fathoms long, but perfectly gentle.
They roam the shallower waters like sea-cattle

and graze on the waving flags of kelp.
At the slightest wound their innards will flop

out with a great hissing sound,
but they have not yet grown to fear mankind:

no matter how many of their number might be killed,
they never try to swim away, they are so mild.

When one is speared, its neighbours will rush in
and struggle to draw out the harpoon

with the blades of their little hooves.
They almost seem to have a grasp of what it is to love.

I once watched a bull return to its butchered
mate two days in a row, butting its flensed hide

and calling out quietly across the shingle till the darkness fell.
The flesh on the small calves tastes as sweet as veal

and their fat is pleasantly coloured,
like the best Dutch butter.

The females are furnished with long, black teats.
When brushed hard with a fingertip

even on the dead
they will grow firm and the sweet milk bleed.

from Journal of a Voyage with Bering 1741–1742
by Georg Wilhelm Steller

The Ugly

I love you as I love the Hatchetfish,
the Allmouth, the Angler,
the Sawbelly and Wolf-eel,
the Stoplight Loosejaw, the Fangtooth;

all our sweet bathypelagic ones,
and especially those too terrible or sly
even for Latin names; who staple
their menfolk to the vagina's hide

like scorched purses, stiff with seed;
whom God built to trawl
endless cathedrals of darkness,
their bland eyes gaping like sores;

who would choke down hunger itself,
had it pith and gristle enough;
who carry on their foreheads
the trembling light of the world.

And What is It?

And what is it?
Listen and I will tell you. It is an animal. It belongs to a phylum. It came from an ancient sea, an egg; it swung through the pitch of a mother's womb. Once upon a time it breathed with gills. It is a bitch that will become a dog, a hen changed into a cock; it is the little girl who grows up to be a boy; a princess who would be king. It procreates and becomes as a multitude. It seeks the warmth of the herd yet desires to be alone.

What is this thing made from?
Yes, I know what it is made from. It has been made from salt, cartilage, epithelium, fur, enzymes, water, bone; its eyes face one way, towards its food. It has teeth for tearing and jaws for mastication. Each limb is decked in vestigial claws. If you ask me who made it I will tell you God made it.

What is it called?
Well I can tell you its name. This is its name: it has a common name and a Latin binomial. It has an official name and it has been granted an individual name. Perhaps it turns its head when this name is enunciated. And it has a secret name for itself that it mouths without breath at times of a certain nature.

But what does it do?
What it does is this: it walks upright, but it may crawl on four legs, or hang by its limbs. It flies on fins that trawl the air; it pulls itself towards sunlight, scuttles towards stones. It takes itself a mate – occasionally for life, but more often for a shorter period of time. It smells of itself. It can briefly gallop. It burrows and ascends. It swims when there is a need for swimming. It lifts an opposing thumb and touches this thumb against a fingertip. It does this again. It is both known and unknown.

Does this animal make a sound?
Yes. It makes for itself the sounds of many calls. I have often heard them. It calls out even towards the emptiness. Listen now: it grunts; it whimpers; it whines; it snarls. It sings and all the other species listen.

Where is it now?
Here it is that has stumbled in through a door of an empty house. Whose home is this house, I ask? No. I do not know. I do not know this house. This animal is stationed before a window of the house. The window contains an interesting prospect: such a great shelving perspective of similar houses and their shadows and a falling of rain.

What is it doing now?
Come with me and we shall see what this animal is doing. Come along with me now and we shall see.

Glen Dye

by that flinch in the Water of Dye
where its wersh soul swithers
through the Bog of Luchray
and on towards the Dee,
there runs a certain gentleness
of ragged stonework in an old sheep fank,
where a flush of broom pushes out;
and if you happened to lie in its doubtful lee,
come early spring, you might just hear
the wind go clambering through, fluting
a note or two from a threadbare melody,
for nothing but its own sake.

For Lucie

born 5 December 2005

How apt it was we named you
for the light: no more than a small light, mind

– a spunk; a spill; a stub of tallow
cradled against the draft

while our stooped shadows lengthen
and fall away behind.

Here's to you, then, and to us,
to your world and to ours.

We raise you towards the dark.
May you make of it something else.

The Lily

after Donatella Bisutti

Mair o a concept than a common flooer,
I daurdna pu the lily, that gaes
as the altar-cannle's metaphor.

An yet, as in the hert o a'thing pure,
Sae likewise wi the lily, whase
Sulphury yallow pollen bides its oor.

Promise

and the word lost for a single breath, as I lie against you; I promise everything that ever was will grow alive again: the first man in his sudden ignorance spits a sour apple whole, turns to her, who will be no more than an ache in the bones of his heart, as you are for me; for this breath, in my arms, the rain falling through the moment's light; then let me rest for one day, for the strength to unmake myself; the beasts of the earth and the great whales, to shift continents into oceans, to take down the firmament and blink into the failing light, the failing darkness for a moment's breath, a moment's touch, brushing your heart like this, as all things fall back into themselves, leaving nothing in the beginning but the word

The Garden

for Erika

Just for a quarter of a day, I'd have you
follow me through the smoking willow-herb
and my father's garden's half-seized gate,

down to that place where the knowledge
of almost everything comes undone
in the powdery ceanothus shade;

where the apple goes withering back to blossom
in your palm, and the serpent, on its hind legs
in the shadows, leaves off whispering.

Tin

*(the can opener was invented forty-eight
years after the tin can)*

When you asked me for a love poem,
(*another* love poem) my thoughts
were immediately drawn to the early days

of the food canning industry –
all those strangely familiar trade-names from childhood:
Del Monte, Green Giant, Fray Bentos, Heinz.

I thought of Franklin and his poisoned men
drifting quietly northwest by north
towards the scooped shale of their graves

and I thought of the first tin of cling peaches
glowing on a dusty pantry shelf
like yet-to-be-discovered radium –

the very first tin of cling peaches
in the world, and for half a century
my fingers reaching out to it.

Mangurstadh

I send you the hush and founder
of the waves at Mangurstadh

in case there is too much
darkness in you now

and you need to remember
why it is we love

Exile

The heart, that other place, its people, ever since the war, whole continents adrift; rain falling, ash and dark; all borders distant or forgotten, all passports burned, all leave abruptly cancelled, all rumours true; and how small it is, you know, that place, and so little cared for: its children stolen, its people subjugate; and now so few, let me say, with everywhere strangers on the move; and yet despite it all, despite the hunger and the summary injustices, despite the stones I threw, still they came on, wherever I went, those ones remaining, hands lifted and empty, still they came after me and they asked – imagine this – they asked for you.

Vitruvian Man

There was a time I tried picturing
the circumference of the soul
but the best I could manage

was a shimmery, milk-blue sun,
an oversized thought-bubble,
a zero with my height

which immediately reminded me
of that hoop he once transcribed
through a sweep of his sepia arms,

as he reached out beyond
the trammel of himself and caught hold
of nothing with both hands.

Blue

Blue: sweet colour of far away,
the colour of farewell,
the colour I remember

from your eyes.
A childhood blue once trembled
where the city stutters

into dusty scrub
and empty marshalling yards.
The last grim veil

of innocence was blue.
If I were asked to construct
a world that wasn't there

I'd make its every surface
scrupulously blue, and you
the only resident.

Stranger

Today, I am a new man,
a stranger in the town that bore me.

How simple it is to become a ghost –
just one word, one gesture, and we slip

through the fretwork of other people's lives
as easily as water through a stone.

Just for today, if I were to pass myself in the street
I wouldn't even raise my hat, or say hello.

Silence the Colour of Snow

Silence the colour of snow
settles against everything we love –
the late, startled flowers, the roadside stones –
all edges softened, all calamities blurred.

Why do you accuse me of never talking with you?
You know, they used to say that
if every tongue in the world were stilled at once,
the common silence would translate itself

to a snow that even our summer winds
could never drive away. Hush now, not another word.
Look! High over the frozen roofs,
my answer hangs and falls, that six-fingered star.

Remember those Wild Apples

Remember those wild apples
we would gather in the autumn, stained
with a half-faced blush, or the viridescent
shadow of a vanished leaf?
They clung to the early cold like a young girl's heart.

Grandfather said they were all seeded
from that first tree God espaliered in Paradise;
its fruit so bitter, even Adam felt compelled
to spread softened honey on the flesh
before he could savour exile, and the world.

A Westray Prayer

i.m. Mike and Barbara Heasman

Let us now give thanks
for these salt-blown

wind-burned pastures
where oatgrass and timothy
shrink from the harrow of the sea

where Scotland at long last
wearies of muttering its own name
where we may begin

to believe we have always known
what someone in his wisdom
must have meant

when he gave us everything
and told us nothing.

Grain

What was his name again – that fisher lad
dragged under with his fankled nets –
him that the fishes hooked and filleted?
I often wonder if the irony of it all amused him
as he left off from kicking against the dark, and drowned:
not (as his mother always feared), to be lost at sea, but found.

Tell me you've never seen a hangman hung,
nor laughed at the dying tenor, topped by his own song;
nor stumbled across a baker's corpse, rising like dough;
nor wept with the weeping ferryman while Charon
gummed his coin. Friends, we're all done for by the things we do.
If I were a farmer, I'd shrink from the ripening grain.

Island Song

I cannot see my mother's face;
no longer know my father's name.
It's the forgetting of the world
keeps me sane.

A stranger's laugh, a neighbour's death;
my wife's despair, my daughter's grief.
It's the forgetting of the world
gives me breath.

The hungry, old, surrounding sea,
heaves at a field's worn edge in me.
It's the forgetting of the world
sets us free.

Noust

Noust in the grass
grass in the wind
wind on the lark
lark for the sun

Sun through the sea
sea in the heart
heart in its noust
nothing is lost

Yesnaby

Not one of us will live forever –
the world is far too beautiful for that.

When my children ask about the War, I'll say:
'I once watched as columns of retreating cloud

burned in a haar of gulls and dust, off Yesnaby;
and I survived.'

from *The Golden Mean*

The Matchsafe

If you must carry fire, carry it in
your heart – somewhere sheltered but hidden,
polished by hands that once loved it.

The lining may be scorched and blackened
but only you must ever know this.
That easy hush you sometimes hear at night

as the darkness stirs in you, is not
the accustomed ache of blood, but a flame
shivering against the wind –

a meagre flame seeded long before you were born
which you have always known must be kept
burning forever, and offered to no one.

Abaton

(from the Greek a, not; baino, I go)

Let's head for a place, neighbouring and impossible,
that city neither of us has ever found;
it swithers somewhere between elsewhere
and here, anchored to the leeward dusk
fettered in cloud.

Look how it flourishes in decline –
no buttresses, no walls, no astragals,
only those luminous avenues of weather
gathering the cluttered light like window glass,
all furnished in the traceries of wind and rain.

A Pint of Light

When I overheard my father say
it was his favourite drink, I closed my eyes
and imagined his body filled with a helpless light.

Years later, I watched him pour out
the disappointing truth, but still couldn't let
that image go: he's trailing home from the pub

singing against the dark, and each step
he steps, each breath he breathes, each note he sings
turns somehow into light and light and light.

Self Portrait in a Dirty Window

after James Morrison, 'The Window 1961'

Don't grumble if this window grants
you only what you see in it.

If you must have light, step out into the world.
If you need shadow, step out into the light.

For once, there is no weight in detail. Who cares
if that's an oily handprint, a belaboured

field or far-off hills? The dirt stain of uncertainty
is all that matters. It fills the room

with neither light nor dark, but the promise
of meaning, which, in itself, means nothing

though it's what you came here for.

Algonquin

for GH and RS

Each dusk is the final dusk. Late mists
forget themselves above the lake.
A crowd of hemlock, shoulder-close and motherly
whispers as its own reflection drowns.
Somewhere not here, a loon calls
out the word for darkness twice,
then turns into the silence and its song.

I kneel where the water frays, and from my hands
build the cracked prayer of a cup.
Let me drink once more; just a little –
one mouthful, one sip would be enough.
Just this time let my hands not leak.
Let them be brimming when I raise them
to my lips, like this.

Ill Will

So. First night of the filling moon
I took me to that spoiled oak, skewed
on its fold of hill above my father's farm.

This left hand hefting his pigman's maul
and under my tongue an old King's penny
vague with spending.

Watched while the sparling moon kicked free
from a trawl of cloud, swam on. Then hammered
the penny to its rim in the faulted grain

and wished down the worst on him by three times
wishing it: *'Tree, by your own dead hand,'* says I,
'wither that blown onion in him no one calls a heart'.

All the path home the stink of night
in the yarrow and dwarf butterbur. Shriek
of the hen-owl restless in her nothing.

Days passed; something he couldn't rage against
whittled him to a skelf, laid him out hushed
and bloodless; grew him his stone.

All this in the month that wears my name. Meanwhile
I followed the ploughshare's hunger through his fields.
Whistled in the old mare's wake. Tasted coin.

Song for a Swift

be owl
my oldest night

be wren
my selfish grief

be gull
my restlessness

be lark
my disbelief

be hawk
my hidden path

be dove
my weary fist

be swift
my only soul

my only soul
be swift

Humpback Embryo

Field Collection, South Atlantic Ocean 1949

Big as a dead man's foot, but closer
to tripes or dough than meat.

Just to be sure, they folded her around herself
head-down in formalin. Her one brief sea.

Note that fluke-stump nicked by her mother's
flenser's blade; the flipper's grace.

Day after day, she grows the milk bloom of a thing
that never moved in cold, green, deepening light;

like most of us. The eye-slit weary, delicate,
beyond insult and closed against our looking.

The Flight into Egypt

after Policarpo de Oliveira Bernardes

Like so much of the Bible, it's predictably domestic:
just a family on its way somewhere, skirting
a thread of towns. Everything is rumours of blue,

because they are in history. No one has courage
enough to look ahead. Joseph glowers
at the chafing calf-boots he bartered for in Bethlehem.

Mary pretends to doze, her fingers locked
around the swaddle. Even their guardian angel
has turned to look back – his know-all smile

encompassing the dusty road, Judaea
diminishing and the almost-new-born who stares
complacently over our right shoulders into today.

Only the old donkey gazes towards Egypt; head down,
ears back, grudging a burden that is worth so little
and a pointless journey he knows has barely begun.

Blossom Street

All that awful mess still lies ahead of him of course:
the silly posturing and bombast, those terrifying
stylish uniforms, the sticky end. For the time being

he's sitting by his mother now her illness has finished
its work. The sickroom carpet ankle-deep in his mediocre
sketches of her, endlessly rehearsing every incidence

of light – all those angles and shadows suffering worked
into her, as if somehow one loss might be lost in many
versions of itself. The traffic dims to a respectful hush.

Echoes skitter in the stairwell, then the impatience of a single
knock. Yes. The time has come to put the pencil down.
From this day forward, the only pages will be blank pages.

The Skylark

*'Again and again it would try to hover over
that miniature meadow . . .'*

One square of turf to floor
my cage, one daisy opening,
one little sun against the sky,

one cloud, one thread of wind,
one song to hang
like nothing over everything.

Amber

Some wounds weep precious through the generations.
They glaze and harden, heal themselves into history.

What was mere sap matures like blood in air to darken
and burnish. To change into something useful, almost.

The Tsar had a whole room built from hurt but it was stolen
and buried. Sometimes the grim Baltic rolls the scars

to shape those jewels women love to wear; especially
treasured where they hold a thing that was living once,

something with quick, venated wings which happened
by and thought the wound looked beautiful and sweet

and that, like other wounds, it should be acknowledged
somehow and, if only for a moment, touched.

The Lost Boy

i.m. Alexander Glenday, died November 4th 1918

November,   and nothing said.
The old world   whittling down
to winter.   Ice on my tongue:
its wordless,   numbing welcome.

We bloody   believed in war
once; we cheered   when our children
sailed off for   the Front. But now
all language   fails me. Listen:

'Army Form   B. 104.
November   1918.'
'. . . a report   has been received
from the Field, France . . .   . . . was killed in

Action.' There.   Alexander
has been killed –   my couthie boy.
Nineteen, looked   more like fourteen.
They told me   his howitzer

was shattered –   a shell 'cooked off'
in the breech,   and the blast tore
them apart.   They were too keen
of course, boys   blown to pieces

[113]

with that Great   War days from won.
Boom. And gone.   I'm a blacksmith.
I've seen what   white hot metal
makes of flesh.   My own wee Eck.

I'm to blame.   I was the fool
who signed, and   him still far too
young. Fifteen!   His mother flung
her mug at   me, mute with rage.

Each morning   she makes his bed;
lays fresh clothes   across a chair.
She'll not speak   his name again.
Her stare is   a hard, black sloe.

If fine rhymes   rang like iron,
hammered bright,   hot with meaning
they might weigh   more in my heart.
Brave songs don't   bring the dead home;

they damn them   to cross that dour
black stream where   yon pale boatman
waits and foul   foundries spit and
silence is   their only song.

When we go   to his grave, I'll
bring sorrel,   because I know
the dead are   always drouthy –
their dry mouths   clotted with dust.

I'll say sorry   son, this plant
slakes only   the one, small thirst;
may its brief   white blossom
linger upon   your grave, like snow.

The Big Push

after Sir Herbert James Gunn, The Eve of the Battle of the Somme

Would you believe it, there's a bloke out there singing
'When You Come to the End of a Perfect Day'.
His audience, a sixty-pounder crew, stand round bleeding
from the ears. The Boche are all but finished, apparently –

I heard they're packing old clock parts into trench mortars
now, for want of iron scrap. Some wag quips that next time he's
sentry and hears the plop of a *minenwerfer* tumbling over,
he'll not blow the alarm, he'll shout: *'Time, gentlemen, please . . .'*

We laugh and for one heartbeat forget to be afraid. Bravery
and cowardice are just two workings of the same fear
moving us in different ways. The 8th East Surreys
have been given footballs to kick and follow at Zero Hour;

it's to persuade them from the trenches lest their nerve fail
as they advance on Montaubon. I've watched men
hitch up their collars and trudge forward as if shrapnel
and lead were no worse than a shower of winter rain.

This afternoon a few of us went swimming in the mill dam
behind Camp. Just for a while to have no weight, to go drifting
clear of thought and world, was utter bliss. A skylark climbed
high over the torn fields on its impossible thread of song:

'like an unbodied joy.' I don't know why, but it reminded
me of the day we took over from the French along the Somme;
it was so tranquil, so picturesque, the German trenchworks crowded
with swathes of tiny, brilliant flowers none of us could name.

I believe if the dead come back at all they'll come back green
to grow from the broken earth and drink the gathered water
and all the things they suffered will mean no more to them
than the setting-in of the ordinary dark, or a change of weather.

The Grain of Truth

Grows poorly in rich soil. Ripening
demands an exceptional season.

Blights more readily than us, even.
Sow it, you'll reap a fine harvest of sorrow.

Each head clings grimly to husk and chaff,
mills the stoutest millstone

to a gritty pebble, kills all yeasts,
sulks in the oven like its own headstone.

So never offer me something
I cannot refuse and expect thanks.

Don't bring me this gift then
ask me why I cannot thrive.

Northeasterly

Driven by sleet and hail,
snell, dour and winterly;

it fills the unwilling sail,
empties the late, green tree.

Something unknowable
lodged in the heart of me

empties itself and fills
Like that sail. Like that tree.

Only a leaf for a sail

and before us, look, the impossible ocean of it all;

squall and storm;

      lash and flail;

the unnavigable, the hungry, the whole perfect

unstarred bleakness of the world,

as though a dark

we had always feared had grown real and cold and tidal,

and the lifted

green-black

ragged face of its hand to pull us,

            pull us down,

and what chance would you say we had,

                so small,

only the two, my love, just me,

        just you,

but give us a leaf for a sail, and suddenly, somehow,

everywhere's possible.

Fireweed

I'm old enough to remember how dangerous
they were, those steam trains butting the weather
south of Forfar, heading for the big smoke.

They would seed sparks among the dropped coals littering
the ballast by the Seven Arches, sweetening the shale for weeds.
Even as we speak the willowherb is hitching upwind

through the decades; it feeds on old burnings,
hungry for nitrogen. At Doig's Farm, their purple heads
crowd above watermint and nettle, or lean out over

the slackwater pools to marvel at themselves – tall, aristocratic,
raised out of last year's waste, abandonment and fire.

Monster

'I have no doubt of seeing the animal today . . .'

I miss it all so much – family and everything.
Father in that lab coat fathers wear;
always too close, always too distant,

always too keen. You may have heard –
my mother was the product of unmentionable
absences and storms; my siblings

a catalogue of slack, discarded failures.
We are all born adult and unwise;
don't judge me too harshly.

Which of us was not cobbled into life
by love's uncertain weathers? Are we not
all stitched together and scarred?

Step forward any one of you who can say
they are not a thing of parts.

The White Stone

when you take it
in your hand

it will weigh smooth
and hard and cold

as the heart once did
long ago

before it was first
touched by the world

British Pearls

'Gignit et Oceanus margarita, sed subfusca ac liventia . . .'
(Tacitus Agricola 1:12)

British pearls are exceptionally poor.
They can be gathered up by the handful wherever
surf breaks, but you'll find no colour, no vitality, no lustre
to them – every last one stained the roughshod grey
of their drab and miserable weather.

Imagine all the rains of this island held
in one sad, small, turbulent world.
I can hear them falling as I write. British pearls
are commonplace and waterish and dull,
but their women wear them as if winter were a jewel.

Windfall

What is love if it is not an unravelling
against the dark? In the moonless field
between house and river, remember

how you stood with your arms
wide to the night, under every tumid
star, waiting for one to drop.

The Darkroom

i.m. WK

If I am the one who is said to be
alive, and you the other, how come it's me
who ends up trailing along behind

as you stride ahead, humming
to yourself, crossing from shade to shadow?
Every morning I wake

longing for you to long for me again;
to dawdle, to loiter, and then – to hell
with the cost, I say – look back.

My Mother's Favourite Flower

This world is nothing much – it's mostly
threadworn, tawdry stuff, of next to little use.

If only it could bring itself to give us back
a portion of the things we would have fallen

for, but always too busy living, overlooked
and missed. So many small things missed.

So many brief, important things.
It is my intention never to write about this.

Elegy

and now that
his song is done

open your hands
there can be no

harm in that
let the notes go free

let them become
ash in the wind

gone back
not to nothing

no
to everything

The Walkers

As soon as we had died, we decided to walk home.
A white tatterflag marked where each journey began.
It was a slow business, so much water to be crossed,
so many dirt roads followed. We walked together but alone.

You must understand – we can never be passengers any more.
Even the smallest children had to make their own way
to their graves, through acres and acres of sunflowers
somehow no longer pretty. A soldier cradled a cigarette, a teddy bear

and his gun. He didn't see us pass, our light was far too thin.
We skirted villages and cities, traced the meanderings of rivers.
But beyond it all, the voices of our loved ones called
so we flowed through borders like the wind through railings

and when impassable mountains marked the way,
soared above their peaks like flocks of cloud, like shoals of rain.
In time the fields and woods grew weary and the sea began –
you could tell we were home by the way our shadows leaned.

We gathered like craneflies in the windowlight of familiar rooms,
grieving for all the things we could never hold again.
Forgive us for coming back. We didn't travel all this way
to break your hearts. We came to ask if you might heal the world.

from *mira*

don't wait

you promised me don't wait for the sun to rise don't wait for
those early clouds to turn from ash to gold don't wait for the
winter sycamore to fill with light don't wait for the sea to wake
or sleep or speak don't wait for the dead you promised me

don't wait

a
tissue
of lies and a tissue
of lies and between them
where the heart should be
that spatter of scorched
seed your mother *don't do*
as i do warned you not
to eat

the only
poem a wasp
can write is round
as a paper moon; look
at her, chewing out her life
in syllables of spittle and regret
desperate to have it done with before
the summer fades and oh how furious she
grows, how furious, with all that wealth
of silence still to be gathered in,
and so very little
time

its astonishing: despite
everything you've taught
yourself about the moon and
all you've read of scars and
silences, to hold it in your
hand and recognize how
wonderfully small it really is,
no weightier than a fairground
token or a well-spent coin, and
yet to sense, from the soles of
your feet to the last hair on
your head, every ocean, every
sea, every puddle and every
drop of rain lean hearkening
towards you.

oceans
and papery
deserts built from
nothing but song

always louder at night
like those ivory flowers
which open only in darkness
so that their voices

i mean their scent
might draw
down the
stars

hush now
its nothing

only the woman
in the moon you hear

all stone and dust and
silhouette   left out there

so far from
the world because

of the things
she sang

even
if it were true
as the old fable goes

it was only his rib
she was built from

her heart
was always
her own

my aunt
whom tb and
the streptomycin
all but killed

          survived

to run her index finger
round the bone-white scar
of my sister's bcg

          like the
pale wax seal on
a promissory note
or letter of
love

o
love my
perfect circle
built from nothing
filled with all the
things i'll never say
always beginning
and always
beginning

you

offered
him a
        silver coin

        that
ferryman whose name
you didn't catch

                then
made him promise
never to

bring you
back

one
face the

worn king
dead and all but

          smiling

the other   a ship

          a ship in the wind

a ship   in the wind
sailing

nowhere

forever

dear
mother
sit up straight
and pick the clot of

earth from your mouth
then tell us what it was
you saw that night preening
the darkness from itself

that made you
forever after
close your
eyes

hush
now it's
only my old
dad's anxious ghost
come back again

fuck off i tell him
leave me in the dark
i'm here and me and
perfectly alright

then wake to
my own hand
fumbling for
the light

what
ever will become
of us

and
what can we possibly
do

when
we've too many
words

and
so little to say
or

so
much and too
few

nothing

>is too costly
>to be borrowed

nothing

>is too pressing
>to delay

nothing

>is too heavy
>to be carried

nothing

>is too difficult
>to say

that shape that coin that
solitary overarching light that
other solitary light that empty
plate that sound my mother
made when

that heart that torus with a
heart that thing that found the
tiniest thing that vowel filling
the throat with our own spent
breath that breath that *quelle*

surprise that form like nothing
nothing makes that world of
dust and world of flame that
little weathered world that
sadness barely spoke that petri
dish that honest seed pod in
the bitter frost that

space where letters gather
clear of words that shape the
dead make in the dancing air

Uncollected Poems

An Empty Bowl

for Erika

Love, here's an empty bowl for us.
Our firmament. We'll fill it with a gloaming
of hazel and gean, the shout of a fox

in a blue field and that brightest,
indomitable star that was never a star.
Remember how it burned a hole

through the darkening air? Henceforth,
let every suffered night founder
like this: so full of itself it is empty,

threadbare with constellations,
seeded with the light of its own undoing.

Least Willow

'The thing to be known grows with the knowing.'
(Nan Shepherd)

Least willow will cling to the slightest grief:
a half-sheltered crevice in the high granite

or shallow seam of grit; and following five seasons
of storm and ice and mirk, when at last

the burn is hurrying so clear no one can find
the words for it, will lift from its gloss of leaves

an indifferent bloom, so easily overlooked;
in gratitude for this stone and this hill

and this nation and this earth – intricate, fragile,
unforgiving, and all we will ever need.

A Riddle

57.835037, −5.626664
for Erika

Part dust, part stone
part distant flame

part bitter wind
part summer rain

never to die
yet not quite living

without leaf or bloom
but always blossoming.

Yesterday's Noise

'how sweet is yesterday's noise.' Charles Wright

Now, when your eyes settle to the dark in here, you'll see her better:
look, she's more of an interference with the light than ghost,
that Walker's factory girl. She lives on the factory floor now,
stacking and loading plastic trays of angel cakes, pigs' lugs,

vanilla slices, macaroons. Look how she goes about her empty
business in a closed-down warehouse, wiping machinery,
washing the waste from the belts. You'll notice she never looks up,
perhaps for fear of seeing us. Who knows? We're her ghosts after all,

waiting to be born. But just for now, she's as real as we are,
working her youth out, joking and laughing with her girlfriends,
thinking of Friday when they'll pour out, like something spilled
across the cobblestones, into Sugarhouse Lane. Somewhere out there

the boy, long dead, who, when he kissed her first, tasted a day's work
sugaring her cheeks and lips and smiled; told her he would eat her up,
she was so sweet. Neither would mind how soon the dusk came down,
their own breath losing itself in the white breath of the rain.

The past was listening and swallowed them, they were so sweet.
Look, sweet is never white, is always anything but refined;
sweet isn't gathered nicely in a silver bowl, sweet like all other flesh
is grass, is tall and rank, is the massed purple stalks hacked down,

then crushed and pulped; is good people placed on scales and
sold for three pence a pound; sweet is as useless as burning straw,
sweet is bagasse, or jaggery, its amber hefted bulk; sweet is the small hell
of the boiling house; the tar pits of molasses; sweet is the dark that clings.

Clings to this place and to its ghosts, its old cast iron pillars
gleaming slicker than treacle, glazed with the past. The past is sweet,
and always lasts. Nothing stays nothing here, the past is never lost,
is never late. You take one step too close, your hands will stick to it.

An Apple, a Boulder, a Mountain

after Edward Steichen

This is what I shall bring him.
I will say, take it from me:
it has become heavy and my arm aches.

Eat it, and I need never
carry it again. I offer it to you
as an emblem of love.

It is an apple, a boulder,
a mountain. Weigh this and you
will have weighed the world.

Blackthorn

Snow that year, though less than a whisper – barely enough
to build, with numb hands and a dark hour's work, not
a snowman, but a snow child; a shapeless thing that lived

just the one bleak night in its crib of winter grass before
it weathered back to rain. Its frown a broken hazel twig;
for eyes, two perished sloes that seemed to focus far

beyond our gaze: Christmas and a stranger on the way,
Boxing Day's excess, Hogmanay tinkling a lonely glass,
then far-off Easter with its promise of cruelty and cruelty

undone; and out there somewhere, someone alone
stumbling upon the old blackthorn lit with a thousand blooms,
all different and identical, filling the lane, filling the air,

filling her heart with a light like, yes, you've guessed it, snow.

Bird Sighs for the Air

sunt lacrimae rerum

Bird sighs for the air? There are those
who would insist air sighs for the bird.
All that bluster and expanse nothing more

than a reaching out towards the least
fraction of itself – a flicker of wren through
summer briar, one note from a firecrest's song.

Everything is the shape of the longing
it was built to hold. Even the olive wears
the curve of the stone it carries in its heart.

And you? Your empty arms confess
to everything they held once and then lost,
or longed to hold but never came to hold.

Your arms, filled, all those things
you are holding now – things you desired,
things you have yet to lose.

Birch Wind

Just a touch of air in the birch trees
lets them sing their ragged moment;
catches the trim of the early leaves,
passes on; likewise all the stuff of
me is stirred, lit and purposed, all
my being someone, grown. This
breath of air through the reed of a
tapered leaf, is a shred of song half
sung to everything but itself; always
almost heard and almost always
gone.

For My Wife, Reading in Bed

I know we're living through all the dark we can afford.
Thank goodness, then, for this moment's light

and you, holding the night at bay— a hint of frown,
those focussed hands, that open book.

I'll match your inward quiet, breath for breath.
What else do we have but words and their absences

to bind and unfasten the knotwork of the heart;
to remind us how mutual and alone we are, how tiny

and significant? Whatever it is you are reading now
my love, read on. Our lives depend on it.

ACKNOWLEDGEMENTS

I would like to thank my wife Erika without whom none of this would have mattered.

Grateful thanks once again to Don Paterson, my editor at Picador, for his perceptive comments, his long-term encouragement, and most of all for his dogged patience.

In memory of the late Harry Chambers of Peterloo Press, who published my first two collections.

Previously uncollected poems have appeared in the following publications and anthologies:

The *Bookseller*; *Christmas Garland* (Candlestick Press); *Coast to Coast to Coast*; *Into the Forest* (Saraband 2013); *Irish Pages*; *Magma*; *Photoukindia*; *Poetry Ireland*; the *Scores*.

'Birch Wind' was broadcast on the BBC Radio 4 programme *A Susurration of Trees*.

'Yesterday's Noise' appeared as a filmpoem by Alastair Cook.

The poems from *mira* were inspired by 'Untitled (Disks)' by the Brazilian artists Mira Schendel and published as a limited edition pamphlet in collaboration with poet and artist Maria Isakova Bennett.

'For My Wife, Reading in Bed' first appeared in *Off the Shelf: A Celebration of Bookshops in Verse*, edited by Carol Ann Duffy (Picador 2018).

Finally, I would like to thank Creative Scotland (previously The Scottish Arts Council) for their support over the years.

www.ingramcontent.com/pod-product-compliance
Ingram Content Group UK Ltd.
Pitfield, Milton Keynes, MK11 3LW, UK
UKHW012345080625
459466UK00001B/19